 Published by: **The Bluecoat Press**, Bluecoat Chambers, School Lane, Liverpool, L1 3BX

Photographs appear courtesy of the Board of Trustees of the National Museums and Galleries on Merseyside
Front cover: Pier Head c.1959; *Back cover:* Pitt Street tenements c.1935

Designed by: Graham Nuttall

Printed by: G.Z. Printek

ISBN 1 872568 41 6

A Liverpool Album

Photographs from the Stewart Bale Archive at the National Museums and Galleries on Merseyside

The Bluecoat Press

Introduction

Born in 1899, Edward Stewart Bale was still a child when he and his parents emigrated from Australia to Britain. His father ran an advertising agency; however he experienced great difficulty in commissioning illustrative photography of a sufficiently high standard. Consequently, when Edward was of age he was trained as a photographer. As additional employees were taken on, the photographic side of the business expanded and Stewart Bale Limited began to earn a reputation as specialists in the fields of architectural, commercial and shipping photography.

> **"His name is associated with a quality of performance which has never been equalled in the field of photography in which he specialised."** (The British Journal of Photography – volume 91,13/10/1944)

The firm operated out of Liverpool from about 1911. In the early days, Bale's situation in such a busy port, with the hinterland of the industrial north-west certainly contributed to their success. Many of the world's great shipping companies were based in Liverpool and Stewart Bale was able to encroach upon a market previously monopolised by the London firm of Bedford Lemere. Indeed, the Stewart Bale client record stands as a 'Hall of Fame' of Liverpool's industrial heritage with customers such as the Cunard Steam Ship Company, the Alfred Holt and White Star Lines, Cammell Laird Shipbuilding Yard, BICC and Meccano. Stewart Bale was also appointed Official Photographer to cover such projects as the construction of the Mersey Tunnels, and the building of both the Liverpool Anglican and Metropolitan Cathedrals.

Stewart Bale photographers continued to use large format cameras long after most commercial photographers had switched to more modern equipment. The larger cameras could combat the distortion often experienced in architectural photography. Such large format cameras took glass plate negatives which produced exceptional results but required great discipline on the part of the photographer. Indeed Edward Stewart Bale demanded no less, yet he was a kind and thoughtful man, always referred to as 'Mr Edward', who regarded his staff as a second family.

Robert (Jack) Hughes secured an apprenticeship with the firm in 1933. He remembers that the staff at that time included Frank Holding Elsam, senior photographer; William Plighting, photographer and specialist retoucher who was awarded the Order of the Nile for aerial desert photography; Noel Gresford Hartley; Leslie John Cooper; and Robert Wilson Mann, artist and ambidextrous lettering expert. The office was managed by Walter Gerald Kay, who also served as Mr Edward's secretary.

Although based in Liverpool (a London office was opened later; evidence exists of its operation between 1949 and 1970) the firm covered a wide geographical area. Superb craftsmanship and technical excellence led to commissions being received from almost anywhere in the country at a time of considerable industrial, commercial and social development. Life was exciting for young apprentices at Stewart Bale, frequently they were sent to photograph the construction of the great Cunard liners, such as *Queen Mary* and *Queen Elizabeth* at John Brown's Shipbuilding Yard on the Clyde; and to cover speed trials off the Isle of Arran. Jack Hughes remembers that in forty two years at Stewart Bale every assignment was a story in its own right, but was particularly privileged to photograph the opening of Queensway, the first road tunnel under the Mersey.

Less enjoyable assignments, however, included the recording of the devastation inflicted on Liverpool during World War II (as featured from page 32 to 37). There was also 'accident' work for the Admiralty, such as the *Thetis* submarine disaster in 1939.

Stewart Bale had founded a company widely regarded as the best of its kind in the country. When he died in 1944, his son Ted took over the company for a short period before he himself died. Hilda Bale-Williams, Ted's widow, then gained control.

During the War, most of the staff had either gone into service or been laid off, until 1946 when work resumed. However, post-war Britain was a very different place. Although the company continued to prosper throughout the 1950's and 60's, in spite of an earlier wage dispute which had led to the resignations of three senior members of staff, the industrial profile of the country was shifting. After enforced cutbacks, Stewart Bale Limited ceased operation in the early 1980's.

National Museums and Galleries on Merseyside purchased the collection of surviving Stewart Bale negatives in 1986. Housed within the Department of Archives at the Merseyside Maritime Museum, the collection of approximately 200,000 negatives is currently being documented, cleaned and re-stored to archival standards. An index of the Archive is being created to facilitate use of the images by members of the public, academic and commercial researchers alike.

"Thus his work will indeed live on" (The British Journal of Photography – volume 91,13/10/1944)

KAREN HOWARD – Curator of the Stewart Bale Archive

Enquiries should be directed to the Curator of the Stewart Bale Archive,
c/o NMGM ,127 Dale Street , Liverpool L69 3LA. Telephone: 0151 478 4695 Fax: 0151 478 4790

Princes Dock c.1954.

Brownlow Hill photographed from the Adelphi Hotel 1931.

Excavations for the foundations of Liverpool Metropolitan Cathedral 1931.

The Queensway Mersey Tunnel, traffic experiments at Old Haymarket 1932.

Lime Street c.1950.

Victoria Street 1936.

Victoria Street/Stanley Street 1936.

"The Legs of Man" public house, Lime Street 1935.

Fruit barrows alongside T.J. Hughes Department Store, Stafford Street c.1951.

Pier Head, Liverpool c.1959.

The Landing Stage 1937.

*The launch of **Mauretania II**, Cammell Laird, Birkenhead 1938.*

*The launch of **Mauretania II**,*
Cammell Laird, Birkenhead 1938.

***H.M.S. Ark Royal** in the River Mersey 1954.*

*The launch of **Mauretania II**, Cammell Laird, Birkenhead 1938.*

The salvage of* Empress of Canada *in Gladstone Dock 1954.

The shipment of Liverpool's last working tramcar to the USA c.1958.

Opening ceremony of the Queensway Mersey Tunnel, Old Haymarket 1934.

Ceremonial laying of the foundation stone of Liverpool Metropolitan Cathedral 1933.

Construction of Liverpool Cathedral 1927.

Construction of Liverpool Cathedral 1935.

Canadian troops, Liverpool 1942.

Riverside Railway Station 1945.

Canada Dock 1944.

Cammell Laird Shipbuilding Yard, Birkenhead 1940.

Detail of war damage panorama (opposite).

War damage to Liverpool city centre 1944; devastation around the Victoria Monument 1944.

Bomb damage, Church Street 1941. Bluecoat Chambers can be seen in the background.

Bomb damage,
James Street Station 1941.

Bomb damage, Bootle 1941.

Bomb damage, Bootle 1941.

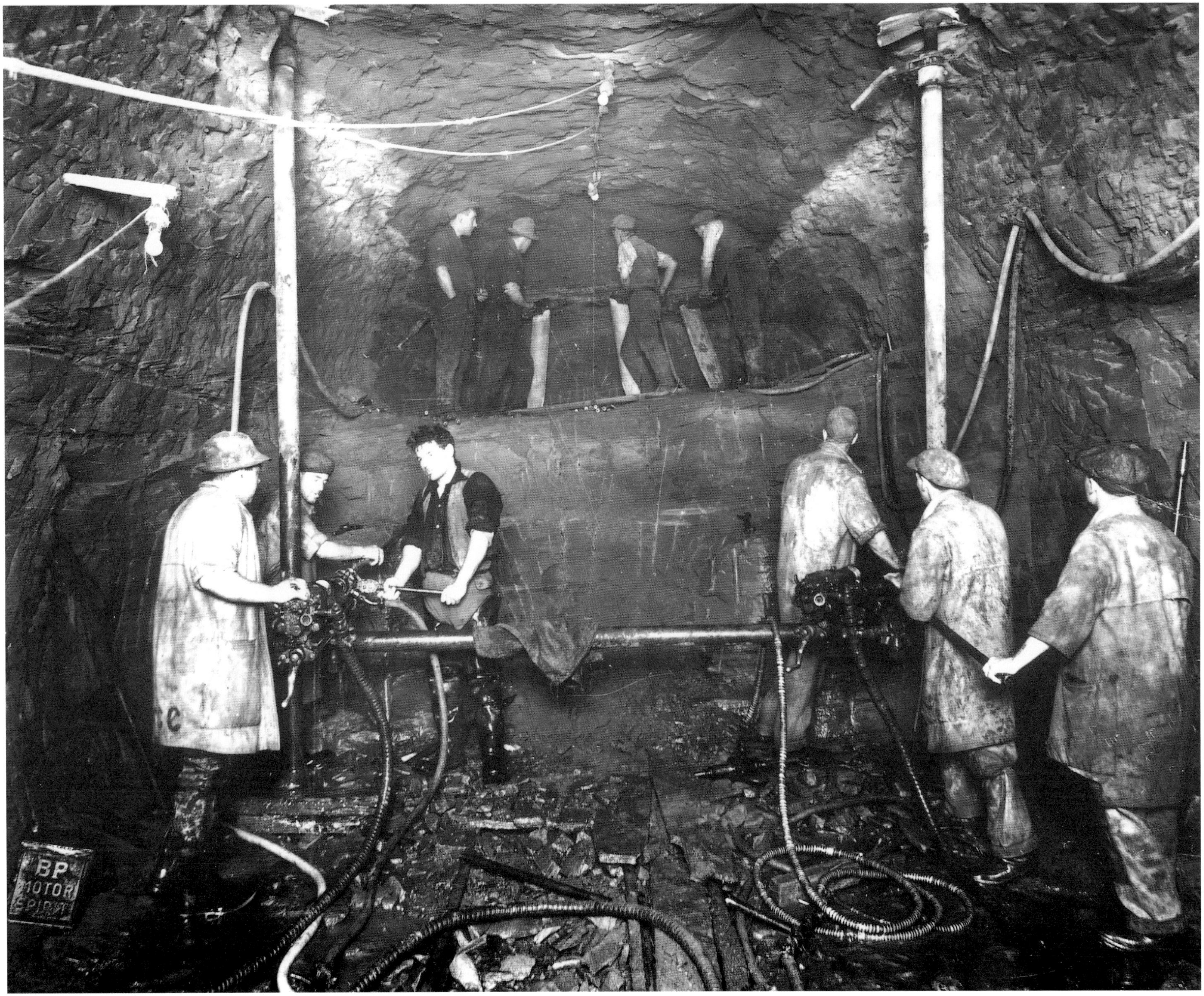

Queensway Tunnel, workers at the Rendall Street heading, Birkenhead 1928.

Queensway Mersey Tunnel c.1931.

Weighing tobacco leaf, Stanley Dock Warehouse 1937.

Dunlop Rubber Co. Factory, Walton 1940.

United Co-operative Laundry, Norris Green 1935.

Meccano Works, Binns Road 1932.

Diphtheria inoculations at a Birkenhead clinic 1935.

Mill Road Maternity Hospital 1946.

Haggis window display, Cooper's Store, Church Street 1930.

The Cigar Room, Cooper's Store, Church Street 1930.

Woolworth's Café, London Road 1931.

Window display, Woolworth's Store, London Road 1931.

Rushworth & Dreaper's Store 1936.

Cooper's Café, Church Street 1932.

Liverpool Personal Service Society Christmas party, Victoria Buildings 1945.

Christmas party for children of employees of BICC, Prescot 1959.

Train enthusiasts 1951.

Florence Institute (The "Florrie"), Mill Street 1946.

Deck Games aboard* Queen Elizabeth *1946.

Opening ceremony, New Brighton Baths 1934.

Musicians at the Locarno Ballroom, West Derby Road 1950.

Orchestra, Reece's Café 1931.

New Gaumont Cinema, Dingle 1937.

Forum Picture House, Lime Street 1933.

Abbey Cinema, Wavertree 1939.

Curzon Cinema, Prescot Road 1936.

Trocadero Cinema, Camden Street 1932. The cinema foyer was decorated as a GWR [Great Western Railway] station to publicise the film "The Ghost Train".